Phoenix

Poems and Prose

By Merton Poets and Whatley Writers

FOREWORD

2015 sees the 25th anniversary of the founding of The Merton Poets (originally the Wimbledon and Merton Poets). We meet at 8.00 pm on the first Tuesday of every month in the former coffee shop of the Methodist Church in Worple Road, Raynes Park. (a two minute walk from the station)

All are welcome to come along, read a poem they have written and have very constructive but friendly criticism of it. The standard is mixed with many of the poets having had volumes of their work published, most having had the odd poem printed in a magazine or two, all are encouraged.

Whatley Writers is a spin-off group where poems and prose are read and discussed. The members take it turn to host these evenings.

This volume gives a sample of the work of both groups, we hope you enjoy it. If it inspires you please come along to a meeting for a warm welcome.

We thank Alban Low for the illustrations and Russell Thompson for the cover. We also thank Geoff West for assistance in proof reading.

For further information email Russell Thompson on zznsh@yahoo.co.uk. Or simply come along on the first Tuesday of any month,

John Grant
George MacGillivray
Lesley Rootham
Editors

Contents

Solitary Watch	Zena Henderson	1
The Blacksmith of Kabul	Alec Linstead	1
The Dismantling	Russell Thompson	4
How to Accept Sympathy	Rosanne Gomez	5
Time	Zena Henderson	6
Exceptional	Veronika Marsh	7
Preparation	Paul Roden	8
The Canterbury Cabby's Tale	John Grant	8
Lumbar Support Cushion	Patrick McManus	10
Join the Library	Patrick McManus	10
One time	María José Fanjul Rodriguez	12
"Age of Gold"	María José Fanjul Rodriguez	13
The Fluffing	María José Fanjul Rodriguez	14
Page Three Girl	Keith Drake	16
Gallowglass	Humphrey Aylwin-Selfe	17
Visiting Dad	John Grant	18
Clutter	Christine Sherlock	19
The Dinner Party	George MacGillivray	20
Memories	George MacGillivray	21
Garden visit	John Grant	22
Wish You Were Here	George MacGillivray	23
The Waterfall	Ann Vaughan-Williams	24
Cycling	Ann Vaughan-Williams	25
Tourist in the Scottish Highlands	Andy V. Frost	28
Kite and I	Andy V. Frost	29
N.P.L.	Christine Sherlock	30
On Return from Summer Holiday	Ann Vaughan-Williams	30
Mistress of the web	Jo Silver	32
In the High Street	Veronika Marsh	33
April Holiday	Paul Roden	34
On an Unknown Shore	Humphrey Aylwin-Selfe	35
Little Red	Lesley Rootham	36
Actress	Keith Drake	37
Revenge (Diary of an Oyster)	Lesley Rootham	38

Time after Time	Geoffrey West	39
Poetry Workshop	Humphrey Alwyne-Selfe	42
Getting Your Own Back	Gary Taylor	43
I Am a Cat	Olga Harkness	44
A Cautionary Tale	Rosanne Gomez	46
My Operation	Gary Taylor	48
Polling	Gerald Hildreth	49
Buddhas	Robin Vaughan-Williams	50
Drip	Russell Thompson	50
Liftshaft on Beulah	Russell Thompson	52

Solitary Watch

He watches in the park
Seasons as they flow
A happy young couple
Turn to three,
Then a family of five
He sees them on the slides,
the swings, the climbing frame.
But they don't notice
As time passes by
The empty cold bench
Soaking in the rain.

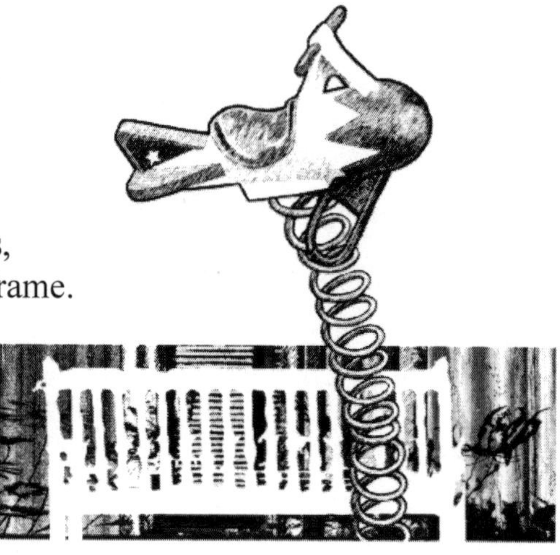

Zena Henderson

The Blacksmith of Kabul

For Lawrence Rootham and his company

1.
He tells me he has passed "The Physical"
and there's "The Interview" four days from now.
He's so brimful of hopes he's irrepressible.
He's run his mile, and he's been very quick;
his time was excellent the sergeant said,
for now that is, but not at Catterick.
Still he'll be near his Mum, ten miles away,
and after twelve weeks' basic he'll have leave
to visit home upon that final day.
They'll wave him off, and maybe plant a kiss
smelling their child, the way all parents do
that atavistic pang so hard to miss.
I give him my best hopes, then catch my breath
knowing this blacksmith's lad's too close to death.

2.
He dreams of horses and the Cavalry
in dashing ambuscades upon Kabul.
He'll be the blacksmith whose tenacity
will prove a modest backup to success.
They have not warned him of the blood and shit,
the battle flashbacks in war's total mess.
He'll pat his favourite stallion to one side
and grip the hoof while fitting on the shoe,
then watch it stepping out with champing pride.
His horses will not fail. Imans will swoon
to see those fleet feet bring sweet peace again
and with him there all will be over soon.
He'll dream of horses.
No.
Perhaps he'll rave
shrapnelled by car bombs
to a foreign grave.

3.
There's a last station that he will not see.
Brookwood, where pines lift heads of solemn green
and youth sleeps wrapped in stilled serenity.
Each time the train stops eyes are always drawn
to wonder at this large memorial ground
that lies well tended. Not at all forlorn;
But with its rank on rank of military
as poignant as those other cemeteries
the vast parade grounds way across the sea,
Just past Deepcut where the paddocks show
the latest Arab stallions bought by those
who value oil monopolies and never know
the dreams of soldiers,
but complain the charge
of wars when audited
are much too large.

4.
So he will go in ignorance to feel
just for a little he is part of life,
but life that means to see his blood congeal
shattered and hanging in a car to leave
only a memory, more dear than summer rain.
His dad will aim at boasting as they grieve.
'Our lad did what he thought was right.
.... He did!'
And Mum will wonder and not say a word.
And all the others too will say "Our kid........"
for sentences though formed will trail away
on anniversaries when memories will come
and hopeless they'll sigh
"...........What can one say?"
"To Jacko"
But the glass will barely rise,
nor will the heads be raised,
eyes avoiding eyes.

Alec Linstead

The Dismantling

My father looks over the brim
of his glasses and says “There’s
a book here – somewhere
– from the sixteen-hundreds.”

“Time we threw it out, then,”
says my Mum, a wedge
of between-the-wars children's
annuals under her chin.

She waddles them away, turns
them into another room’s problem.
My dad and I are hunkered
down or on sets of steps,

undoing screws. His every
movement sags with wondering
why we’re doing this at all –
dismantling shelving. Curses

filter through his Jimmy Greaves
moustache, leaving only consonants.
Fifty years of screwdrivers
sulk in a red, plastic trug,

to be tried and retried on over-
zealous screws. Now and again,
the agony of cracking woodgrain.
I sketch it all in biro: fudged

3D and notes-to-self – “This side
to wall’ and ‘Slat attaches here” –
for when the decorating’s over.
Dad, ushering a freed-up upright

against the wall, says "I reckon
I've got four-and-a-half thousand
books here, you know." Mother
enters, grabs up a coverless,

broken-backed thing, and:
"I suggested he sort out some
he could bear to part with.
So he did." She holds it above

her, flaps its pages. "This one."

Russell Thompson

How to Accept Sympathy

I could feel their pity all around me,
warm, close and clinging
as a soft unwanted blanket.
I would have liked
to tear it from me
and fling it in their faces –

But swaddled in the tight silk
cocoon of their sympathy,
I merely thanked them
and accepted
the superior hot-water bottle
of their patronising.

Then, when they had gone,
I undid the stopper
and poured it down
the plughole.

Rosanne Gomez

Time

How to fit it all in
First it was playing and school
Time for homework, time to go to bed
Then came studying
Lectures at 2, library at 4,
Film at 7, pub at 10.

After this
Shopping, cooking, housework.
If only she had a second to spare.
Then early morning feeds, nappy changing
Car runs, helping with homework.
A full circle no less!

Now she sits dozing,
Watery slit eyes
Under reptile lids
Drooling and wrinkled
Her own armchair at "Cedars Haven"
She pretends not to see
The nurses winking slyly
As she repeats a story once again
Now at last she has all the time in the world!

Zena Henderson

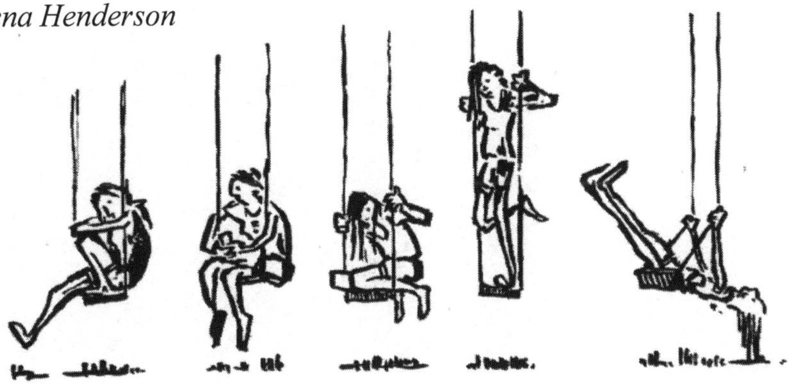

Exceptional

At first glance it wasn't exceptional
that puddle
stretched in guarded blue
between the woods
and the midriff of the path
lapping up to the mud
on its tail ends

Edging closer it took you aback
that puddle
was an eye into another universe
still reflecting in its outer iris
trees and branches leaning over
curious of an image of themselves
amongst the vanity of clouds

The middle was an opening
a centripetal vertex
in vitreous layers
of mirrors and dark light
that had no end
and drew you
into a limitless parallel

and the fearless jumped

Veronika Marsh

Preparation

All season long the leaves grow thick
with the thought of birds
and what they will make of themselves
when they harden and mature:
mimic sparrows scuttling across paths,
flock like finches in poplar branches,
shape their wings like crows
to skim along the hedges,
or shorten their span to imitate
the scalloping flight of the robin.
Taking short days from the long
they have time to prepare their ribs
struts and webbing, making ready.
It's their one and only chance.

Paul Roden

The Canterbury Cabby's Tale

Inspired by *The Merchants Tale* from *The Canterbury Tales* by Geoffrey Chaucer

I had that Geoffrey Chaucer in the back of my cab once.
He speaks a little funny and you'd take him for a dunce
until he starts a chatting and a telling of his tales,
talk the leg off of a table, got more spout than whales.

I met him at the station and we got on right away,
told me he's up from Southwark for the day.
I showed him the Cathedral and the ancient Roman wall
and where it's said Kit Marlowe went to school.

Said he'd like to meet some locals, perhaps with a tale to tell,
I took him to The Millers Arms and he got on very well.
He met a merchant banker, who told him of another -
sixty three and a half years old with a twenty year old lover.

He married her and gave her gifts of gorgeous clothes and jewels
but pretty girls can turn the wisest men into blindest fools.
A posh house, a beautiful garden, a lovely place to live,
but it seems the woman wanted more than the rich old man could give.

Damion, the gardener, was a lovely looking lad,
a six-pack and a suntan and a face to make you glad.
He met with May, the pretty wife, behind the old pear tree,
and the saying is true, there's none so blind as those that will not see.

Janus was the old man's name, he could see when the markets would rise,
he simply just refused to see what was in front of his eyes.
But the marriage worked, they were both contented
for to what each wanted the other consented.

Mr Geoffrey Chaucer was happy as a reformed sinner,
"Come on" he said, "you've been good to me, I'll treat you to some dinner."
"I can surely use that story, but I might have to expand it."
And it all worked out so neatly it seemed the gods had planned it.

John Grant

Lumbar Support Cushion

they kindly
bought their dear old
White-haired granny
for her poor back
to ease her pain a
lumbar support cushion
back rest - multi position
in luxury faux sheepskin
but visiting her
late one night
they were rather surprised
to discover her using it
in the missionary position
in flagrante delicto
in front of an open fire
with a young Romeo
and knocking back
best malt whisky
neat from the bottle

Patrick McManus

Join the Library

let's see sir
you wish to
join the library
you state that
your name
is God
also known
as Jehovah, Yahweh
Sovereign of the Universe
The all Powerful

Lord of Lords
and others
but do you have any
proof of identity?
yes I can see that
you have a halo
and can do miracles
thanks for that
my pain is cured
but no sir please sir
do not get agitated
and do not threaten
library staff with
those winged heavies
standing outside
and plague and pestilence
showers of frogs fire
brimstone and treacle
they would damage
our book stock
and no sir
the Four Horsemen
of the Apocalypse
had to fulfil the
same conditions
do you have a
council tax statement?
or driving licence?
or a passport?

Patrick McManus

One time

One winter
We went up the mountain pass.
You started a fire in the ice
And cooked white rice
With the snow you'd melted from the lake,
We weren't cold anymore.
That meal fed me for years.

One year
There were patches of
Green and blue percale
Like corn flowers
And you sewed them into a dress
that danced and showed off summer
when I walked.

The night that father didn't arrive
You sang about bells
Of the moon hiding
Under your bed,
Dressed me in its light
And took me to journey the darkness,

And as I looked at the sky
Feeling your hand in the silence
I knew that we loved each other.

María José Fanjul Rodriguez

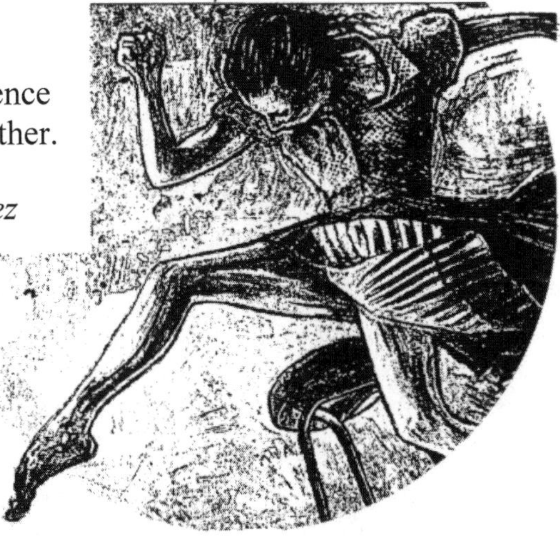

"Age of Gold"

by Shostakovich, Performance by Lisa Batiashvili at the R A Hall

Her armoured prince was that violin,
an average looking instrument,
if you ask me,

but, when she held it in her arms,
it embodied a mythical being
beyond this realm,

A beast of yielding pleasures
that first swallowed her completely
and then every one in that Hall,

each reappearing inside
a Dante-like age of gold,
or was it his ninth hell?

in that trance,
I don't know where
we went,

but in the distance I saw
a higher space above horizons
where all sounds met,

and there was no thing,
but light.

María José Fanjul Rodriguez

The Fluffing

In August, when the sun
is strongest in the mountains,
we changed, came to life,
didn't feel buried by coal mines.

We cleaned every corner,
the dresser drawers, closets,
scrubbed the floors with bleach,
whitened the walls, above all,
we made again the mattresses.

They had become hardened balls of wool lint,
- caked coffins - hurting kidneys of those
who'd slept in them for a year.

This mattress was a sack of cloth
that used to be striped red or blue.
Inside was the fill; straw for poorest.
Kapok, cotton, mainly wool.

The previous day,
we had washed the cloth in the basin,
soaped the wool
in the pools of the sloping spring.
It was time to get on with the fluffing.

We placed the lumpy wool on the floor,
on a site that was paved and well-swept
with brooms made of millet and hemp.
Joy in the streets of communal work!

Each armed with a rod of ash or hazel,
we beat and shook the pile of wool.
The rod dipped in and out hooking tufts.

Break for the pitcher of water or wine,
let the arms off the repetitive task.
The air, thick with dust,
made people sneeze and cough.

Caning after caning, hitting after hitting,
the balls of fluff are broken open, spongy.
The wool is swollen and the tuft is loose and flabby.

The well worked wool is placed
on the fresh fabric of the mattress,
evenly distributed, covered partly
and with a curved needle, we sewed,

threaded the ribbons, clicked eyelets with studs,
so the wool wouldn't roll
when the mattress was moved.

The whole village had opened up,
fluffed, pricked its secrets
and closed again till next August.

María José Fanjul Rodriguez

Page Three Girl

I don't want to topple in a wishing well
Or be polished off by an enemy shell
The way I've lived, I ain't got much credit
If there was curse to curse I always said it
So when the time comes for my toes to curl
Please let me go, wrapped around a page 3 girl.
When I get a hint of that peachy aroma
I'll forget the palsy, oedema and glaucoma
It'll cheer me up, even at arm's length
When I get tucked up by a page 3 wench.
She'll cover my nose with an oxygen mask
Proclaim I'm about to breath my last
Stroke my cheek and the back of my head
Then solemnly announce, he's nearly dead.
But it won't be a clot that stops my heart
It'll be the lingering kiss of a page 3 tart.
I'll smile from deep inside my grave,
When they call me a rascal, immoral and depraved.
At my final address, these words must be heard:
The bugger was found across a Page 3 Bird!!

Keith Drake

Gallowglass

Tooting Bec Hospital. 1992

Life----------carried away
Like charred paper
                    On the breeze

Has gone.

To be slammed in by
                    fast locked doors
Which echo in endless hallways,
In a twilight world
          of hopelessness,
Where by night and by day
Distant, unknown
Cries of pain
Echo with mixed voices,
          Scream,
Is this the end

Humphrey Aylwin-Selfe

Visiting Dad

A car wash drive round the M25,
turn off towards England's Garden
On a pilgrimage to visit my dad
who could soon be heading for heaven.
Although on his own he still lives at home
with his Carry on Jack sense of humour.
Home, hospital, home, with hospice next stop,
he's had heart attacks, strokes, now a tumour.

I get down to the bay – his car is gone.
He shouldn't be driving! Can't have gone far,
he's left a light on and his dog is still there.
Is that a figure, still, in his chair?
I look through the glass but you can't really tell.
I rap on the window and ring on the bell.

I return to my car. I sit. I wait.
I hope he's alright and I'm not too late.
I phone up my sister – 'What shall I do?'
She tells me his car is with twin number two,
so he must be inside. What if he's died?

Supposing he's ill. Supposing he's dead!
My mind bungees back to things done and things said.
To blackcurrants, gooseberries, rhubarb,
cricket and football and fun.
To curtain wire across my arse
and dad having rows with my mum
when the money had gone on the horses
or dogs. But that was a long time ago.

I will have to break in.
No need to I'm told –
Go round the back, there's a box on the wall,
four numbers will give you the key to the hall.
So through the back gate, into the garden,
look in the window into the kitchen.
There looking out is my dear old Dad,
looking at me as if I was mad.

He'd been sound asleep.
The bell didn't wake him and
The dog didn't bark.
I wanted to shake him
But hugged him instead.

John Grant

Clutter

Chris, your house is in a mess
so get it sorted;
all the things you ever bought,
all the things you once were taught,
all that junk mail in your room,
it must be thwarted!

Christine Sherlock

The Dinner Party

Smoke billowed out from the kitchen
The fire alarm went off
The alarm was wired to the station
The fire brigade turned up.

They came walking in with their hoses
Shouting “Where’s the fire”
The hostess pointed to the cooker
And collapsed in a flood of tears

Nothing had gone right for her
Her sauce was as lumpy as hell
Her soufflé had sunk in the middle
And the beef was burnt to a cinder

The bottle of wine had been opened
Ready to put in the stew
It went into the hostess instead
Who cheered up and greeted her guests

The guests looked on askance
As the firemen rolled up their hoses
Poulet a l’Americain was on the menu
or KFC as it’s commonly known

The guests averted their eyes
As the hostess swayed gently before them
They resorted to drinking as well
To stop them from feeling embarrassed

So the party went with a swing
Until it was time for the guests to go home
All the guests suddenly realised
They were drunk and incapable of driving

They all woke up the next morning
The booze had taken its toll
The kitchen was totally wrecked
They couldn't even make coffee.

They groaned as they left the flat
And stumbled their way down the stairs
They resolved to eat out in future
And politely decline invitations.

George MacGillivray

Memories

I don't want to remember you
As you were in old age
Your mind in another world
Which I could not enter.

I don't want to remember you
For your violent outbursts
Your insults to those who help you
Or your complete helplessness.

I want to remember you
As you were when you were younger
Proud and independent
When life was still an adventure.

George MacGillivray

Garden visit

Unaware of my approach
you continue weeding while I watch.
Your slim brown body adorned with a shirt
casually open at the top.
Blue jeans hug your hips.

Eventually you notice me,
greet me with a smile, a sparkle in your eyes.
Your face is lined with years of laughter
and every wrinkle seems
an invitation for a kiss.

You are happy to show me
your beans, carrots, cabbages,
all nearly ready for harvest.
Your hands are rough with toil,
soil darkens your fingers.

I imagine your hands on my body,
mine on yours.
Your mouth on my mouth.
You offer me strawberries.

John Grant

Wish You Were Here

Your armchair is now empty
The one you always used
Your favourite jacket is dusty
The one you always wore

Your ghost is always present
Surprising me at quiet times
And quiet times is all I have
Now that you're gone

All the things we did together
Now I must do on my own
They won't feel the same as they did
Without you to share them with me

Organising the funeral was a comfort
It gave me something to do
It meant I didn't sit thinking
As the silence enveloped me.

I know I must build life again
But how do I do it without you
For now I must sit and grieve
And trust time to heal my wounds

George MacGillivray

The Waterfall

A thunderous noise comes from the waterfall.
Up the rocky side steps invite me to climb.
A railing gives a handhold, sharp with cold
for this rift drops from the glacier above.
Through trees that cling the summer sunshine
flickers: I mustn't be defeated.

The way grows steep, I won't allow defeat,
my senses almost numbed by the dinning falls
tumbling and scouring rocks hidden from sunshine.
I keep on going, it's not that hard a climb.
Turning a corner, a cliff closes in from above,
Buffeted by the wind I shudder with cold.

My body aches, caught in a clamp. So cold.
Need to turn back, but that would spell defeat,
to run away from the force that towers above.
Stooped, keeping steady along the waterfall
on the path chipped from rock I keep on climbing,
cheered by glimpses of blue sky, sunshine

on a day for walking the hills all bathed in sun.
Inside this gorge is icy cold.
I stop to catch my breath. On I climb.
Could not turn back. Shout against defeat,
voice drowning in the clangour of the hurtling falls,
water surging over boulders from above.

No one can see me from below or above
where trees and bushes bask in brilliant sunshine.
The harsh way twists and turns with the waterfall
rolling from the glacier. I'm blue with cold.
The noise envelops; the steepness defeats me.
I will hang on. I am doing well. Such a climb,

but I stay the course, will not forget this clamber
up the zig-zag sides of the split rock. Above,
a dark tunnel appears: I still the echo of defeat.
Continue through darkness into sunshine;
the effort warming me, not so cold; see
a flight of steps at the source of the waterfall.

A fall worthy of the effort of the climb.
I feel so cold, but light filters from above.
I blink in the sunshine, undefeated.

Ann Vaughan-Williams

Cycling

1
I used to love to ride the hill
the beaten red earth road
cycling from up the offices
my long hair streaming in the sun
limbs dark brown
from equatorial heat.
I sailed my bike
past cotton coffee crops
gardens with hibiscus hedges
down to where the tall tree grew
a perch for crested cranes,
their high view in the sky:
they'd see the hills beyond
our green enclave,
my safe Kawanda home.

2
I later leaned into
the biting wind
ripping the land
flattening Norfolk flatter
myself astride
my green bike's sturdy frame
pushing the pedals
over the bumps
of former plough land
lungs at work
to counteract the blast.
At times a tyre went flat,
fixed the nozzle with frozen fingers
fearful of being late for school.
I'd leave the bike
tethered
in the Black Horse shed,
waited for the bus.

3
Some days I'd cycle
to the West Lynn Ferry,
at low tide the mud banks
rose like monstrous sides of slime,
above the boat
wending its *phut-phut* way
inside the heady salt of the sea,
skirted the swirling current
as the Great Ouse
turned
to pour into The Wash.
The rocking boat was lassoed to a stump,
I'd keep my balance, satchel swinging
stepped up the creaky jetty,
mustn't slip;
hurried the narrow lane.

4

I like to watch the cyclists now
in cycle lanes right through Raynes Park.
Some go like wind.
Today a child came flashing past:
reminded me
of freedom in prevailing wind
hands lifted from the bars
the surface smooth,
the jolts of puddles taken,
seat absorbing frictions,
wheels covering distances;
applying the brakes in time,
or maybe not,
sometimes falling off
to tumble into grasses,
lie watching the sky.

Ann Vaughan-Williams

Tourist in the Scottish Highlands

Streams of tea chilled to perfection by Pre-Cambrian Gneiss cubes.

Treacle lakes lapped by shorn or woolly sheep
that proceed to devour anything green that resembles food,
before turning kamikaze and crossing the road.
It is always greener on the other side,
just as someone is passing.

White Van Man has long since changed to Red Van Farmer,
and the Rats that won the race to leave the city
are now Lemmings in search of the highest cliff.

The Sun blinds you around the next bend,
a spotlight for Julie Andrews launching herself over the brow
with arms outstretched like an eagle.
But you never see the lonely goat,
and eagles are rarer than rainbows.

Mountains never seem that high when you're amongst them.
The dilemma of is it mist or cloud is answered,
once you can see clearly again.

And you stop taking photos
when every mountain, glen and loch
looks just like every other
mountain, glen and loch.

Yet,
Just when you think you have seen it all,
You'll reach the nearest horizon
and something new will jerk open your mouth.

Andy V. Frost

Kite and I

These striding winds are all for us
my playful friend.
Take my dreams with you,
soar high and fast,
let this amphitheatre of open air
enfold us

With leashed input,
I'll hold you tight then loose
to make you dance and loop.
You'll be flying, my mind skying,
fuel, for these precious moments,
between us.

We'll relish the twists and turns,
swoop low, climb high,
ride the updraughts,
surmount the sky,
and forget the world,
it can exist for a while,
without us.

Andy V. Frost

N.P.L.

There is something delightfully exploratory
about the National Physical Laboratory.
Always a busy schedule
going on in each module.
Examining, testing,
measuring, weighing,
engaging in mind-boggling experiments
to enhance future experience
in climate, time and travel;
who knows what they'll unravel?

Groundbreaking truths in the field of biology
destroying old wives tales and mythology?

Christine Sherlock

On Return from Summer Holiday

The apple tree is laden and in the un-mown grass
fallen ones make scatterings of red.
My teeth can't wait to crunch the sunned flesh.
I'll not mind brown tunnelled bits
the worm and grub devour.
Juice drips from my fingers.

Dropped apples pecked by birds are strewn inside the flower bed,
some half hidden by plants,
some lodged between rocks
straddled by untended flowers gone to seed.
I search out an armful, cradle the crimson
to my chest.

Wind has blown
the wayward tomato plant
off the low wall where I left it,
into the pond where it rests
lopsided on its plastic plate. I lift the gangly thing
whose fruit are dark green, thick-skinned
spliced and bulbous from uneven waterings
They might make chutney.

Resting on the plinth, half submerged
is not a clod of earth: it has two hooded eyes.
Flattened, like parchment,
the old frog, stares up at me,
pulsing.
He's still with us.

The evening light falls suddenly at eight,
the darkened window holding my reflection
as I empty the suitcase into the laundry basket,
put away the lightweight clothes.
Search out a warmer top.

Ann Vaughan-Williams

Mistress of the web

Miniscule eight legged creature
How you weave
Busy with so much work
Choose a safe place
Your design is so intricate
So fragile, almost invisible
To the eye. One fine thread
To begin with.
Firmly anchored
Between two twigs
Then she knits her
Silken threads, woven so
Carefully. If at first you
Don't succeed, you'll keep
Going,
Spindle, spindle, spin
So many superstitions.
Symbol of luck in Turkey
Knit one pearl. On to the next
Two types of stitches
Round in a circle
She tells her story to me
Like the women in the East
Tell their stories in carpets
The web so finely woven
Soon the winter will come
Your home will sparkle with
dewdrops.
For the world to see.

Jo Silver

In the High Street

We saw each other just past the toyshop
and I knew what happiness was
stretched out my hand – and caught
a world buoyant in translucency
a raindrop universe trembling in my palm
with oceans of colours painting worlds
and centrifugal galaxies dancing in the light

I smiled, it radiated back with a laughter
that disguised an old sadness
of something lost in the needs of the day
where the air hurried past traffic and people
pressing on, ahead, faster, further –
and still the bubble held me in its spell
a silvered clarity showing how to be

A circle of beauty, a question
for me, right here on the pavement
where I stood in adoration, waiting
when, with the mischievousness of an impatient child
the bubble burst
with a spray of fairytale soap and rainbow
and placed a wet kiss right on my nose

Veronika Marsh

April Holiday

You know, she said,
because we are travelling tomorrow,
we will miss the tulips and the iris,
they will bloom and be done before we return.
And the bluebells, too, I reminded her
as if they were essential travel items.
Oh well, she said, some times
some things one just has to do without.
So, instead of the coming adventure
we remembered the sequence of flowering
that lent a fullness to previous springs.

And on the morning when we were to return
she leant across the table on the terrace and said
Do you know? From tomorrow
we will no longer be able to watch the brothers
setting up the tables in the square
or hear the bells at matins
or smell the stephanotis from our room
or see the birds circling over the headland
before they set out to sea.
Oh well, I said, some times
some things one just has to do without.

Paul Roden

On an Unknown Shore

And the company rowed him into the bay,
The land, thickly covered with steep forest
All down to the shoreline
With plunging streams in deep ravines
Which made a mist in this strange exotic place,
There they moored their boat
And carried him, their commander
And their friend
They bore him upon a stretcher
With great dignity
Toiling up through thick jungle
To the summit where they laid him.

For him, there they dug a shallow grave
And covered him with juniper boughs
And delicately coloured flowers from this paradise.

At midnight, under a ghostly moon,
They talked of past campaigns, of victories glorious
And there they buried him with all solemnity
Leaving him with his sword.

They departed with very heavy hearts
And descended to their boat in the bay
And silently rowed, out into the darkness
Leaving Their Commander
Under the stars to sleep.

Humphrey Aylwin-Selfe

Little Red

Little Red wore her very best clothes
She dressed in red from head to toes
To go and see her gran who's sick
Mum baked some cakes and said be quick
Don't linger in the woods today
Stick to the path and do not stray.

Now Little Red once in the wood
Pulled up her pretty bright red hood
And as any clever wolf would know
Our Wolfie knew just where to go
He'd watched her Oh so many times
As he planned his latest crimes.

He took a shortcut to the house
And crept in quiet as a mouse
Then shot upstairs and Gran was gobbled up
Jumped into bed and drank from Granny's cup
With her glasses on her nose
The duvet covered claws and toes
Gran's cap hid the ears upon his head
As he snuggled deep inside the bed.

Little Red knocked and let herself in
Wolfie couldn't hide his toothy grin
They skipped the pleasantries like "What big eyes"
As Little Red had her own surprise
She knew just how the story goes
And slapped him soundly on the nose
Then karate-chopped him across the neck
As Wolfie cried "Oh blooming heck"
"Who taught you all these nasty tricks?"
As she threw him at a wall of bricks.

All that bouncing around shook up his tummy
Until he coughed up poor old Granny
The woodsman watching from the door
Saw Wolfie sprawled out on the floor
"You don't need my help" he was heard to mutter
As his courage began to flutter
Then disappeared into the night
After all he'd had a nasty fright.

Little Red proceeded none too neatly
To skin poor Wolfie quite completely
Then at home drinking tea from her mug
She wriggled her toes in her wolf skin rug!

Lesley Rootham

Actress

You are a natural
When inhabiting others' skin
Convincing from the heart
Not the outside looking in
Ungrabable space
Is nimbly traversed
Red blood pumped through
Languid lines so eagerly rehearsed
The tale you tell is not what is
But magic that can be
For only the brave can respirate
What the dull will never see!

Keith Drake

Revenge (Diary of an Oyster)

Sliding sneakily up beside this lovely lady's shell,
Reflecting shafts of sunlight, I'm on a winner I can tell,
When suddenly in great clouds of sand and weed
I'm torn asunder, deep in trouble, yes indeed.
Dredged up from my ocean home and dumped on deck,
Sized and sorted, packed in ice, Oh blooming heck.
I've heard the stories one too many times,
I know what's coming, it's the end of the line,
But I have a secret that I'm not going to tell
I'll make you pay for sending me to hell!

Soon served up as a seafood dish and placed on your table
In a restaurant with a five-star good food label
A dead eyed shrimp is next to me and a scallop on my right,
I pushed aside a mussel to sit here in your sight!
I watch you smile as you make your choice
And listen to your sensuous voice,
Then down your slender silken throat I slide,
Where sweet revenge will start deep down inside.
You see I slipped from under the sheet of packing ice,
Sat on top of the the box, I warmed up in the sun quite nice.
So now I am an oyster with an extra special bite.
Even dead you will find I can keep you up all night!

Lesley Rootham

Time after Time

When I saw the old lady wandering around the top-storey car park of the supermarket where I'd only been working for a month, I wondered just what I should do.

It was 6 o'clock on a freezing cold winter's afternoon, my shift about to finish. I was worrying about the scaffolding and building work going on at the neighbouring office block above us that seemed to be threatening the safety of our customers. Just this morning a bricklayer had accidentally dropped his trowel from 20 feet above, and it could easily have hit a customer or damaged a car.

The wandering lady appeared to be mid 80s, perhaps, shy, bespectacled, wistful looking, hardly aware of the supermarket bag she was carrying.
"Excuse me madam," I said, walking up to her. "Can I help you?"
"Oh yes please," she looked up at me with eyes that were moist with tears. "I've lost my car. I think it's been stolen. I really don't know what I'm going to do," she said. "I really—"
"—Come down to our office," I coaxed, taking the carrier bag from her. "We can take a look at the CCTV of the car park."
"It's very valuable, you see," her voice was anxious. "A Mercedes. My husband bought it new, not long ago. A month before he died, in fact." The smoke from our breath funnelled up into the sky, and I noticed she was shivering as well as on the brink of tears.
"That's why I came here this afternoon," she concluded, wiping her eyes with a tissue as we sat in the office, watching the screen. "We used to come here every Saturday, my husband Clive and I. And we would always buy a bottle of your own brand *Celebration* Champagne. That's the only thing I bought today. I wanted to take it home and drink it all on my own. And think about Clive and try to remember what our life was like. Just for tonight I wanted to try and recapture the past."

She was crying so much that I didn't know what to do. Then I remembered the whisky bottle in the bottom drawer of my desk, left there by my predecessor. I found a glass and poured her a drink. She took it without a word, and sipped. “You’re kind,” she said to me.

Then, it was the weirdest feeling. As I looked up again at the cars on the CCTV screen, in all the different parts of the car park, I suddenly realised that they were *different* cars to the ones I’d seen just now, when we were walking around up there.

I asked her to wait a moment, then dashed back upstairs.

It was just like before!

No new Datsun in the far corner, as it had been on the CCTV. The elderly Vauxhall I remembered from earlier on was there now in its place.

And then, to my amazement, *I saw it!* The Mercedes, the car the lady had been looking for! I walked up to it, stood beside the passenger’s side door and looked inside.

Then, reflected in the window glass, I saw the lady herself, standing beside the car park’s parapet wall twenty yards away. Her arms were held out to the night sky. I ran headlong towards her, and it was right then that I heard the crash of the collapsing masonry wall above. The landslide of bricks and rubble was everywhere, knocking me flat, sending me sprawling, a vast cloud of debris rising up and swallowing up everything in sight.

I remember a lot of shouting, people running everywhere, and assuring Sean, my young assistant, that I was okay, that I’d moved out of the way just in time to avoid being killed by the vast heap of broken masonry.

The first thing I did when I could walk was make my way over to the parapet wall where I’d seen her about to jump, aiming to haul myself up to look over the top. But I couldn’t do it.

No one could.

The wall rose up sheer for 12 feet, and it would have been impossible for even a professional climber to scale it without a rope. And the Mercedes? It wasn't there either.

I assumed that both the car and the jumping lady, even the different cars I thought I'd seen, must have been some kind of a hallucination, bought on by stress and worry. That was the only possible explanation.

However, as I joined the men sifting through the rubbish, just before we were all told by the emergency services to keep back, I found a carrier bag. I took it away and shook off the dust and debris, then looked inside at the shards of glass that had once been a bottle. One section of the gold coloured label said *Celebration Champagne*. And underneath that it said *Safeway's own brand.*

Safeways? That had been the name of the original store here, yet for 10 years now, it had been named Morrisons, as were all the erstwhile Safeways stores around the country. I looked at the carrier bag. It was a Safeways bag – the familiar red logo on clear plastic that was no more.

Next day I talked to my boss about what had happened.
"Funny, it was ten years ago to the day that this old lady jumped off the roof," he told me. "Really weird, you know I saw her just before she jumped, but I couldn't get to her in time. And I swear she wasn't on her own. There was a man with her. Man of about her own age.'
"What happened to him?'
"Who knows mate? Must have been a hallucination."

Geoffrey West

Poetry Workshop

Absorbing, drinking in
All that is placed about us
Being utterly refreshed.

This is sheer invigoration and exultation
Celebration of being nourished
By like minds, kindred souls.

The magic of good wordcraft
eclectic euphemism, oxymoron
and even bathos
Come to lighten our way.

With all the tools at our disposal
dialogue, essay, precis
parody, melodrama, satire
We observe life.
Some being moulded into verse
With skills of delight
Of sounds and thoughts unheralded
We would certainly put to flight
Any reason to be downcast.

Humphrey Alwyne-Selfe

Getting Your Own Back

SO, she died in this room. Murdered.
Her screams echoed forth but nobody heard her.
He married her for money, it was all that mattered,
took up a hammer and she splintered and splattered.
Then of course there was this dead body to hide,
there was room in the fireplace so he bricked her up inside.
He told everyone she had run off with some man,
then married the parlour maid because this was his plan.

Some years later it was said over a Sunday roast
the couple were startled by the sight of a ghost.
Half her face missing she smiled all demure
was covered in embers, her breath smelt of sewer.
She slammed doors at midnight, wailed in the morning
then was gone in the day when the sun saw the dawn in.
The new bride she went mad and hung herself so
but the man he swore vengeance, that ghost had to go.

Ghost hunters, priests came forth to exorcise
but our heroine she was cunning as she was wise.
She haunted that house, it was hers and her right
but the man wasn't put off, he'd put up a fight.
He wasn't going to leave there and so he did stay,
she kept on a haunting, he grew older and grey.
Then one day on his deathbed she appeared like you do
he died pretty quickly after she callously went BOO.

Gary Taylor

I Am a Cat

I am a cat. All my relatives are cats too. Our main rivals are dogs. Stupid animals – they bark at the moon. How foolish is that? As for their slave-like mentality, always looking for someone to worship or serve – yuk! We cats are slaves to no one, we are superior and we know it.

Dogs are supposed to see everything and let the humans know. They are the guards. Guards? Don't make me laugh. We cats have a far better view, often from the vantage point of roofs, fences or trees. Not much happens without us noticing it, but we get no recognition from people. Dogs get all the accolades, they are just better at promoting themselves with all that barking and tail wagging.

We are sun worshippers. Roofs for us are what the Riviera is for humans. Dogs are very jealous of our ability to climb. One can often see a dog barking furiously at a cat sitting in a tree, sometimes attacking the tree. It makes us laugh.

We cats make good use of humans, but we don't rate them very highly. How could we? They haven't yet learnt to walk on all fours, or how to fall and land gracefully. You can see them tripping over small objects, or even their own feet, and breaking bones. Have you ever seen a cat tripping over its own paws? Never.

Once, being a bit bored, I decided to go hunting. I caught a mouse, and feeling generous, which doesn't happen very often, I thought I would give it to my lady. She is my housekeeper and very handy with a tin opener. She looked as if she could do with some feeding. She had been running a lot, up and down the road as if a Rottweiler was after her. She calls it jogging. We cats prefer to spend our time horizontally. She called me –
"Kitty, Kitty darling, where are you? Your dinner is here, come to your mummy."

It's so embarrassing to be called Kitty, so *common.* My name is Sheba. I dropped the mouse at her feet, it was wriggling and squealing, then pretended to be dead. I kept my paw on it just in case. I expected some praise from the woman, at least a "Thank you". Instead she let out a mighty blood-curdling scream and leapt into the air.
"A mouse! A mouse!" she shouted, stating the obvious.

For a moment I lost my footing and the devious mouse took advantage and scurried away. The woman's fault, I told you that human beings are not very bright. As soon as we cats learn how to use a tin opener we will dispense with them completely.

For the time being I must stay. You see, my brief romance with Marmaduke, the handsome ginger Tom, resulted in my having triplets. They are the most beautiful kittens. Two tortoiseshell boys and a girl. She is red haired like her dad. Gorgeous.

All was well until one day I discovered that my not-too-bright housekeeper had got a dog. A big ugly brute. Not that I ever met a nice dog. This savage dribbles saliva at the sight of me. I had to move upstairs for the sake of the safety of my children. Yesterday I heard him creeping upstairs, panting, smacking his thick lips. I stood my ground, arching my back. I opened my mouth wide, baring my teeth. I showed him he was not dealing with some puny vegetarian. He was just about to snatch one of my youngsters, I shouted: "WOOF! WOOF! WOOF!"

The villain somersaulted down the stairs, landing on his head. I always knew that learning a second language would one day become very useful. But haven't I told you we cats are superior? And of course, very modest with it.

Olga Harkness

A Cautionary Tale

We were bursting with excitement and curiosity – our elder sister Lalitha was bringing a special boyfriend to dinner. "He's the man I intend to marry," she said grandly to me and my younger sister. "He's a captain in the army and very handsome."

The day duly arrived. We two younger ones were allowed to join the dinner party if we promised to behave ourselves. Captain Tissa Balendra did seem very handsome with his curly dark hair and flirtatious eyes. He was very polite and attentive to our parents, and to Aunty Sita who stayed with us. All seemed to go well.

But a few days later I overheard Amma (our mother) conferring in worried tones with Aunty Sita.
"I hear he is a married man with four children! And he is divorced!" she exclaimed. "Such a man will never do for our Lalitha." Aunty Sita agreed with her vehemently.
"Yes, yes, my dear, we can't allow her to marry him." Then I heard my mother say "We must ask Sisil to give him a large sum of money to stay away from Lali."

The next day an ultimatum was laid down to Lalitha. No marriage was to be permitted to such a man, Captain or not. Lali begged and pleaded, and shed a fountain of tears. Poor Thatha (our father) had to be dragged in by Amma and Aunty Sita to reinforce the argument. Finally it was agreed that Lali could go to the School of Nursing up in the hills, to which she had been saying she wanted to go, and that she could have whatever she liked to take with her. As for the Captain, he must have accepted our father's generous pay-off because he never came to our house again.

For her part, Lali seemed pleased and pacified. Everything she asked for was bought for her. We were quite dazzled by the jewellery, the dresses and the sarees that swirled around her like clouds at sunset, as she tried them on. All this to go to a School of Nursing – my sister and I wondered as we gazed in fascination, quite green with envy.

And then she was off, bags and suitcases piled high. We didn't hear much from her, but when we did, it was mostly about parties and dances – precious little about learning to nurse the sick.

Then a small parcel arrived. Amma opened the little box, gave a shriek and fainted. It contained a few pieces of wedding cake from the marriage of Lalitha to Captain Tissa Balendra.
"Run, Amritha," Aunty Sita ordered me. "Get your mother a good tot of arrack. That should revive her." Amma did revive, with much weeping and wailing, to be comforted by Aunty Sita. Thatha retreated to his study and firmly shut the door.

Well, Lali and her Captain went on to have four children too. Then he divorced her, went off and married someone else, and had yet more children. By the time he retired, he'd had four wives and nearly a dozen children. He didn't do much for them, so it fell to our poor father to support a divorced daughter and four grandchildren.

Rosanne Gomez

My Operation

They're going to cut me open
as I lie here on the table
then everyone will peek inside
there'll be gas to keep me stable.

"Pass me the scalpel," said Doctor Doom.
"A wrench, chainsaw and an axe.
This man's insides is a war zone so
deep breaths before attack."

Said Sister. "Well now I'll be blowed,
what's that you're cutting out?
I do believe a Tonka toy
It's a tank for there's no doubt."

"Let's stem all the blood," the surgeon said
the likes he'd never seen.
Here comes some Airfix aeroplanes
and Action Men in green.

Matron then could not believe her eyes
when Sister went out and told her
they scooped out a miniature submarine
and two battalions of lead soldiers.

They groped down deep in all that gunk
that sloshed about and spilled
found several cowboys and Indians
a red plastic sword and shield.

Things were getting most gory
Nurse Nigel said. "I say.
That's Thunderbird one, mint in it's box
I'll put that straight on Ebay."

The surgeons hacked away at bone
They'd wished they had not begun
for next retrieved were bendy knives
a water pistol and laser gun.

The students in their blue op dress
were surprised at every toy
festering deep within my insides
Said. "I must have been a REAL boy."

But Sister then she had to laugh
"A REAL boy is he?
'out comes Barbie and accessories
and a baby doll that cries."

When I woke up and all stitched up
my eyes were big and round
for all around my bed were placed
my long lost toys now found.

Gary Taylor

Polling

So what is your polling test?
What are the market research rules?
Was my Dad a Duke or Dustman?
Neither? What that does tell you about me?
Oh what class are we? Is that your question?
Well you know. We are sort in the middle.
The sort that keeps England going, while some
Play the fiddle are there you say? Or I will not be drawn be on that.

Gerald Hildreth

Buddhas

The doorbell didn't work
so they chucked a buddha through the bathroom window.
The glass exploded like a nightmare in suburbia
like a bruised face.
Someone doesn't like you
and you know what they're thinking
down the footpath behind the petrol station.
The twitch in her eye, it's caused by the draft
as is the angle of her neck and constant sniffing.
Should've got it boarded up quicker
but she's worried about premiums
losing her no-claims-discount.
At least the buddha's unhurt. She's plenty more
in the garden, next to the birdbath, nailed to a tree.
Buddhas on the mantelpiece, the WC
scattered among photos of grandchilden
in the shrine in the conservatory
where the geraniums help focus the mind.

Robin Vaughan-Williams

Drip

Out of kindness, she has taken the less
comfortable end of the bath, and lies
back as best she can. The taps hover
like good and bad angels, one over

each shoulder. And, judging by the look
on her face, the overflow must be stuck
in the small of her neck. The water
laps and recomposes as she shifts weight

from one buttock to the other. Although
the bath's surround is all shampoo
and conditioner in vivid, upright
bottles, there's not so much as might

suggest extravagance. From above, the first
drip falls onto her chest – an intrusive burst
of cold water. She tilts her head and looks
up at the shower, its own head hooked

on the wall: white tiles in perspective
above her – some with fish. She gives
a shiver and goes "brrr" – exaggerating
only a little – as the fitting

drips again. She says "I'm comfortable
now" – being reluctant to get up and grapple
it out of harm's way. And so it goes
on: every splash followed by a pause

that is more annoying, she says, than
the splash itself. The shower attachment
says nothing, and for all I know it will
drip from now until the end of the world.

Russell Thompson

Liftshaft on Beulah

They have stacked up my slates like silver,
they've extinguished my stained-glass door,
they have chiseled the chequered tiling
from the flags of my kitchen floor.

They've bombarded my gothic turret
with a skip and a JCB,
left my liftshaft the last thing standing
in the space where I used to be.

Let the liftshaft stand on Beulah
like the head of a lonely mine,
till the waves wash over London
and the lift comes one last time.

They have taken my terracotta,
they've reclaimed all they can reclaim;
now my inside's become my outside
and my gateposts have got no name.

They have sold off my coalhole covers
to a cast-iron enthusiast,
they've dismantled my mantelpieces,
but the liftshaft was built to last.

Let the liftshaft stand on Beulah
like the head of a lonely mine,
till the waves wash over London
and the lift comes one last time.

Russell Thompson

Index of Contributors

A

Humphrey Aylwin-Selfe
- Gallowglass 17
- On an Unknown Shore 35
- Poetry Workshop 42

D

Keith Drake
- Actress 37
- Page Three Girl 16

F

Andy V. Frost
- Kite and I 29
- Tourist in the Scottish Highlands 28

G

Rosanne Gomez
- A Cautionary Tale 46
- How to Accept Sympathy 5

John Grant
- Garden Visit 22
- The Canterbury Cabby's Tale 8
- Visiting Dad 18

H

Olga Harkness
- I Am a Cat 44

Zena Henderson
- Solitary Watch 1
- Time 6

Gerald Hildreth
- Polling 49

L

Alec Linstead
- The Blacksmith of Kabul 1

M

George MacGillivray
- Memories 21
- The Dinner Party 20
- Wish You Were Here 23

Veronika Marsh
- Exceptional 7
- In the High Street 33

Patrick McManus
- Join the Library 10
- Lumbar Support Cushion 10

R

Paul Roden
- April Holiday 34
- Preparation 8

María José Fanjul Rodriguez
- Age of Gold 13
- The Fluffing 14
- One Time 12

Lesley Rootham
- Little Red 36
- Revenge (Diary of an Oyster) 38

S

Christine Sherlock
- Clutter 19
- N.P.L. 30

Jo Silver
- Mistress of the web 32

T

Gary Taylor
- Getting Your Own Back 43
- My Operation 48

Russell Thompson
- Drip 50
- Liftshaft on Beulah 52
- The Dismantling 4

V

Ann Vaughan-Williams
- Cycling 25
- On Return from Summer Holiday 30
- The Waterfall 24

Robin Vaughan-Williams
- Buddhas 50

W

Geoffrey West
- Time after Time 39